To Kyle
From James & Théa /85

CONTENTS

dog

Elephant

THE CONTENTS OF THIS BOOK ARE ALSO
PUBLISHED IN FOUR SEPARATE TITLES
LISTED ABOVE BY BRIMAX BOOKS LTD.
© BRIMAX RIGHTS LTD 1984. ALL RIGHTS
RESERVED. PUBLISHED BY BRIMAX BOOKS LTD
ENGLAND 1984. ISBN 0 86112 260 7
PRINTED IN HONG KONG

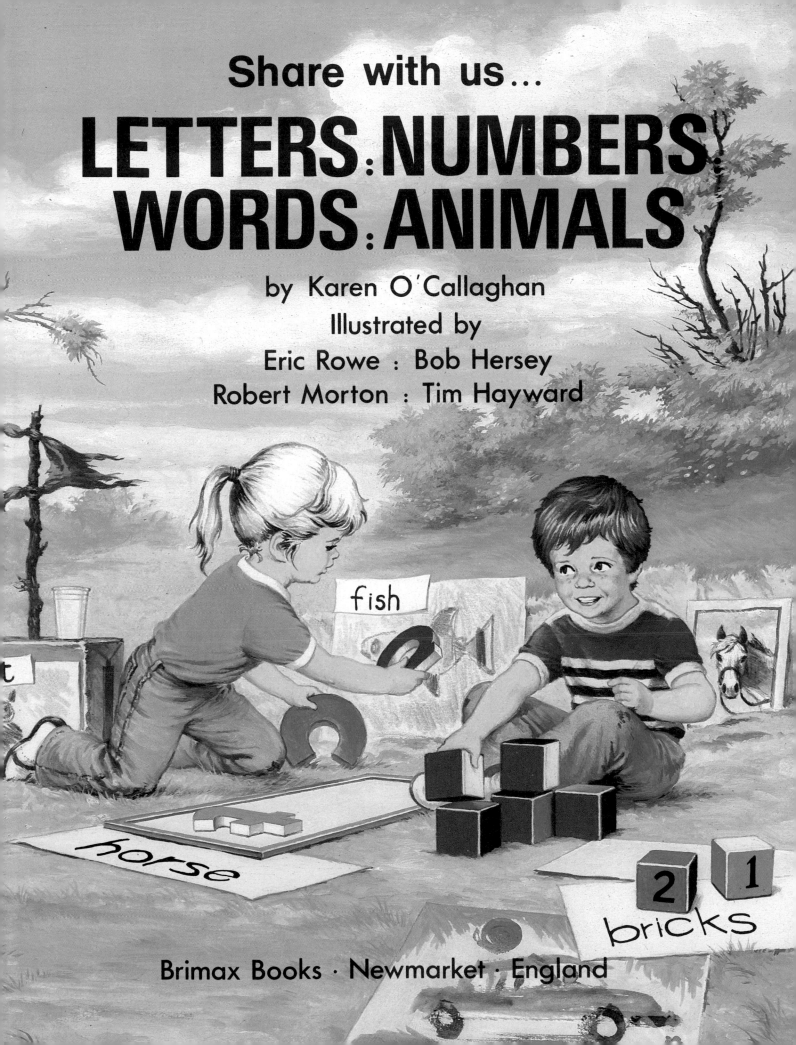

Share with us...
LETTERS: NUMBERS: WORDS: ANIMALS

by Karen O'Callaghan

Illustrated by

Eric Rowe : Bob Hersey
Robert Morton : Tim Hayward

Brimax Books · Newmarket · England

Join in with us !
LETTERS

A Guide to **LETTERS**

LETTERS is designed to be more than an alphabet. Each page offers opportunities to extend the child's awareness, knowledge and vocabulary. The illustrations for each letter of the alphabet are based on actions and combined with descriptive text which introduces other concepts such as, big/little, up/down, rough/smooth.

The letter is printed in red and underlined where it appears in the text. This helps to focus the child's attention on the letter and its position, clearly showing that it is not always an initial sound but may appear in the middle or at the end of different words.

Wherever possible the various phonetic sounds that a letter can make are included, for example, 'e' in eating, 'e' in empty.

Within schools the sound a letter makes is taught before the letter name, as this is an important function of word building.

An adult reading with a child can lay emphasis on the sound of each letter. Extra learning is possible by an adult discussing alternative words that begin with the same sound and adding to the examples given. The two children illustrated, are seen co-operating with and helping each other in everyday situations which can be easily recognised and which enable children to copy the actions and go through the pages by themselves. This can make learning fun.

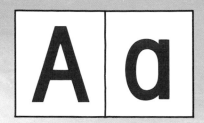

A a

Alex is looking <u>a</u>ll <u>a</u>round for Zoe.

"Here I <u>a</u>m, <u>A</u>lex!"

Point to <u>a</u>ll the <u>A</u>a's.

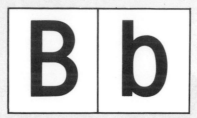

B b

Blow a piece of paper across the floor.
Bend down low and

blow, blow and blow!

Where are the Bb's ?

C c

Curl up tight,
    make yourself smaller.

Can you curl up too?

Can you see the Cc's?

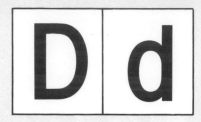

D d

Dancing is fun!

You can do it too!

Alex dances
with teddy

Zoe makes the doll
dance as well!

Where are the Dd 's?

12

E e

Eating ice cream...

Alex is still
eating his
ice cream.

"Mine's all gone,"
says Zoe.
"Now it's empty."

Can you see the Ee's?

F f

Finding the best way...

"These won't fit in," says Alex.

"If we fold them they will fit," says Zoe.
"Folding makes things smaller."

Fold a piece of paper.
Does it get smaller?

Find all the Ff's.

G g

"Go on Zoe, open it!" says Alex.

Who is getting
a present?

Who is giving
a present?

Where are all the Gg's?

H h

Here is Alex holding a box.

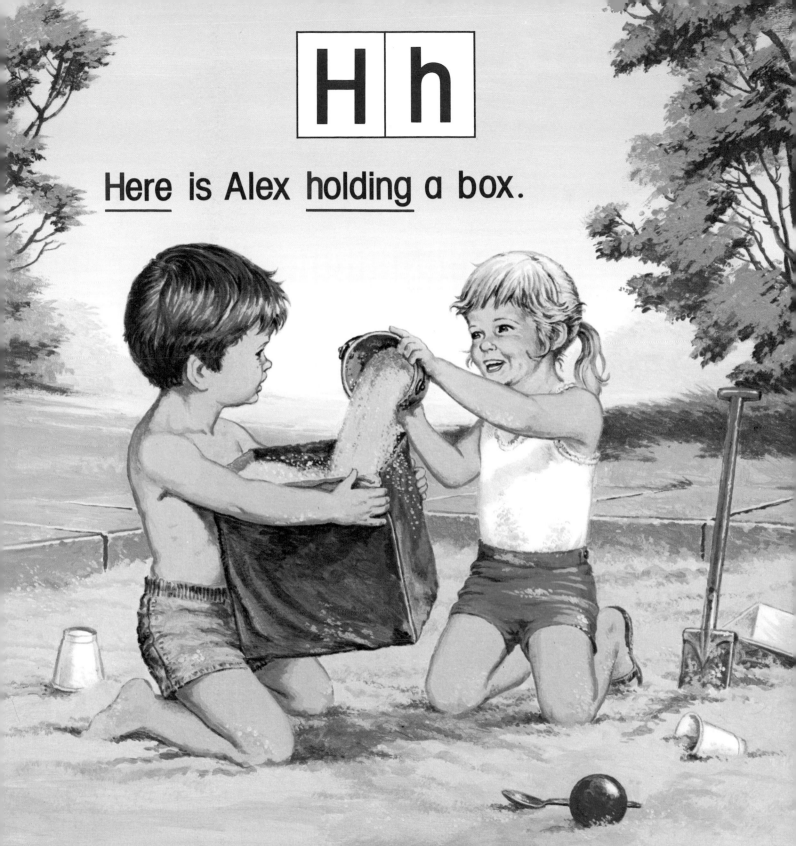

Zoe is helping him to fill it with sand.

How many Hh's are there ?

I i

"<u>I</u> am <u>in</u>side our tent," says Zoe.

"<u>I</u> am <u>in</u>side <u>i</u>t too," says Alex.

<u>F</u>ind the <u>I</u>i's

J j

Join in a jumping game!

Just jump a little - and you're there!

Point to the J j's

19

K k

<u>K</u>ick a ball as hard as you can,
see how far it goes!

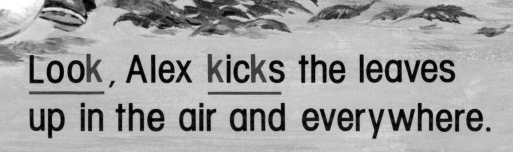

<u>Look</u>, Alex <u>k</u>ic<u>k</u>s the leaves
up in the air and everywhere.

<u>Look</u> for all the <u>K</u><u>k</u>'s

L l

Look at Alex, he is trying to lift the bricks all at once.

Zoe can't do it - she is laughing!

Look for all the Ll's

Mm

Moving about...

"I can see myself
in the mirror."

"When I <u>move</u>,
my shadow <u>moves</u> with <u>me</u>."

How <u>many</u> <u>Mm</u>'s can you find?

Nn

Nod your head to mean 'Yes'...

up

and

down

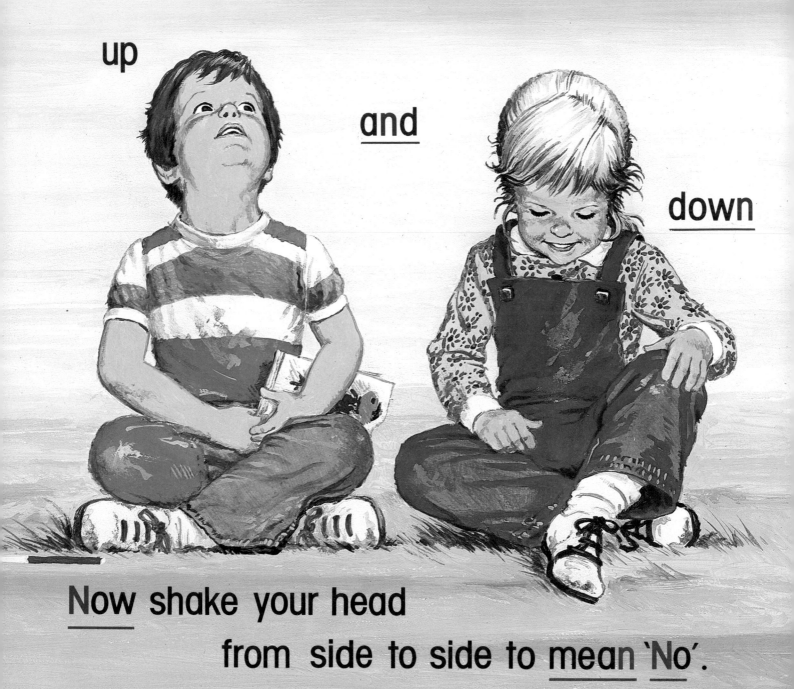

Now shake your head
from side to side to mean 'No'.

Point to the Nn's

O o

"<u>O</u>ve<u>r</u> the chairs we g<u>o</u>!"

"We climb <u>on</u> — and jump <u>o</u>ff!"

P<u>o</u>in<u>t</u> t<u>o</u> the <u>Oo</u>'s.

P p

"Please help me, Zoe.
We can move this together!"

"I'll push."

"I'll pull."

Point to the Pp's

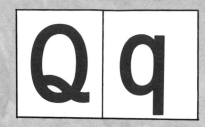

Q q

Quiet! Shh! Shh!

Sit quietly.

What can you hear
when you don't make a noise?

Where is the Q and q?

R r

Run, run as fast as you can.

Round and round and round!

Find the Rr's.

S s

See us sharing something.

"One for you and one for me –
one for you and one for me."

Spot the S's 's

T t

Touch something rough like tree bark.

Look for something smooth to touch
like flower petals.

Touch all the Tt's

U u

"Under we go!"

You must make yourself flat
to go under the chairs.

Can you find the Uu's?

V v

Visiting is fun!

Zoe is going to visit Alex.

Alex <u>wav</u>es, he is
<u>v</u>ery pleased to see Zoe.

Where is the <u>V</u> and <u>v</u>?

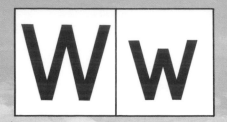

W w

Walking two ways!
Walk with great big steps.

Walk with tiny little steps.

Where are the Ww's?

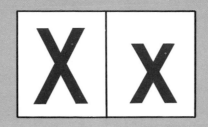

X x

It's e<u>x</u>citing making <u>X</u>'s!

Make yourself look like an <u>X</u>.

Make e<u>x</u>tra <u>X</u>'s with legs and fingers.

Spot the <u>Xx</u>'s

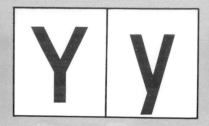

Y y

"<u>You're</u> <u>yawning</u>, Alex," <u>says</u> Zoe.

"I can see <u>you</u>!"

"I'm not tired," says Alex.

"Come and play."

How many Yy's can you see?

Z z

Zoe and Alex are following

a zigzag path.

"Goodbye!"

Point to each letter Z.

Count with us!
NUMBERS

A Guide to **NUMBERS**

These pages are designed to encourage children to observe and count objects within their own environment.

Counting Our Toys from 1–10 is the basic section. Each page shows the number as a symbol, a numeral and a written word—three ways to explain simply to a child the number concept. Colours are also introduced.

Counting at Home/Outside/In the Supermarket—These are familiar situations for children everywhere which stimulate their interest. The child is invited to join in, to find and count using the illustrated number/picture/word key. Repetition of this concept can be used by parents to help children count the numerous objects they can see around them.

The ideas are expanded further to include the order and grouping of numbers, counting backwards, and to show the various activities and games your child can follow.

All children love rhymes. The number rhymes provide a fun way to establish solid and basic number concepts.

Given the examples in these pages, parents can develop new games with their children which involve numbers and counting.

Learning numbers can be great fun.

Counting our toys.

Turn the page and count with us.

one rocking horse

| ● | 1 | one |

two tricycles

● ●	2	two

three boats

| ● ● ● | 3 | three |

four teddy bears

•• ••	4	four

five dolls

| ⁙ | 5 | five |

six balls

| ●● ●● ●● | 6 | six |

seven cars

| • • • • • • • | 7 | seven |

50

eight paint pots

• • • • • • • •	8	eight

nine farm animals

●●●●● ● ●●●●●	9	nine

ten balloons

	10	ten

53

Counting at home.

Have a party and count what you need.

3	forks
3	spoons
3	knives
3	mugs
1	jug

54

Find—

3	bowls
3	apples
3	plates
2	large spoons
1	sugar bowl

Counting outside

Can you find ?...

1		church
2		buses
3		trucks
4		bicycles
5		cars

6		street lights
7		birds
8		houses
9		trees
10		people

Counting in the supermarket

Find and count with us...

1		chicken
2		loaves
3		bags of sugar
4		packets of butter
5		cans of beans

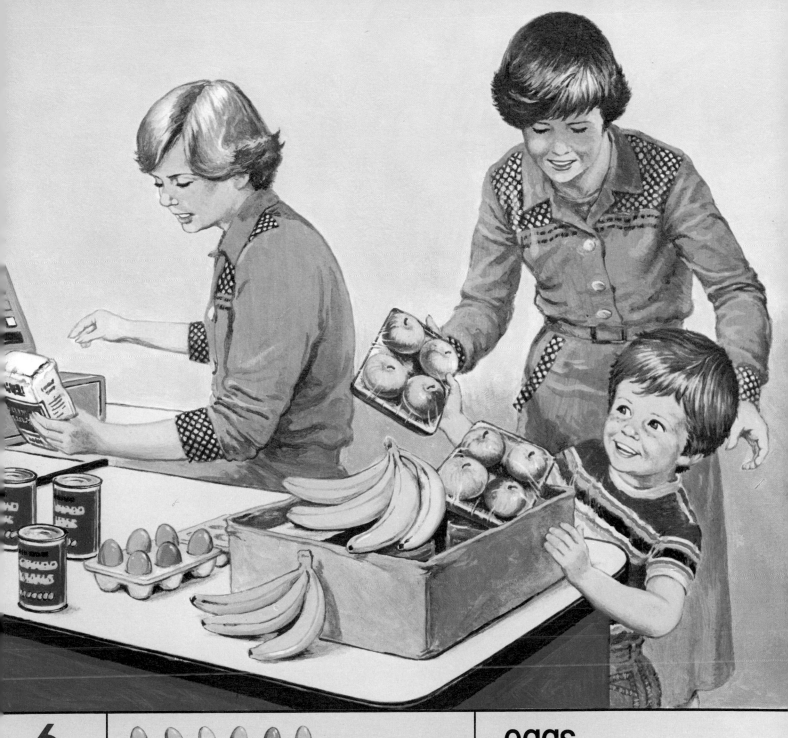

6		eggs
7		bananas
8		apples
9		tomatoes
10		cartons of milk

We can make a number stairway with bricks. Can you?

Count with us up to the top

and back down again.

Counting backwards.

"Help me with the countdown," says Zoe. "Are you ready?"

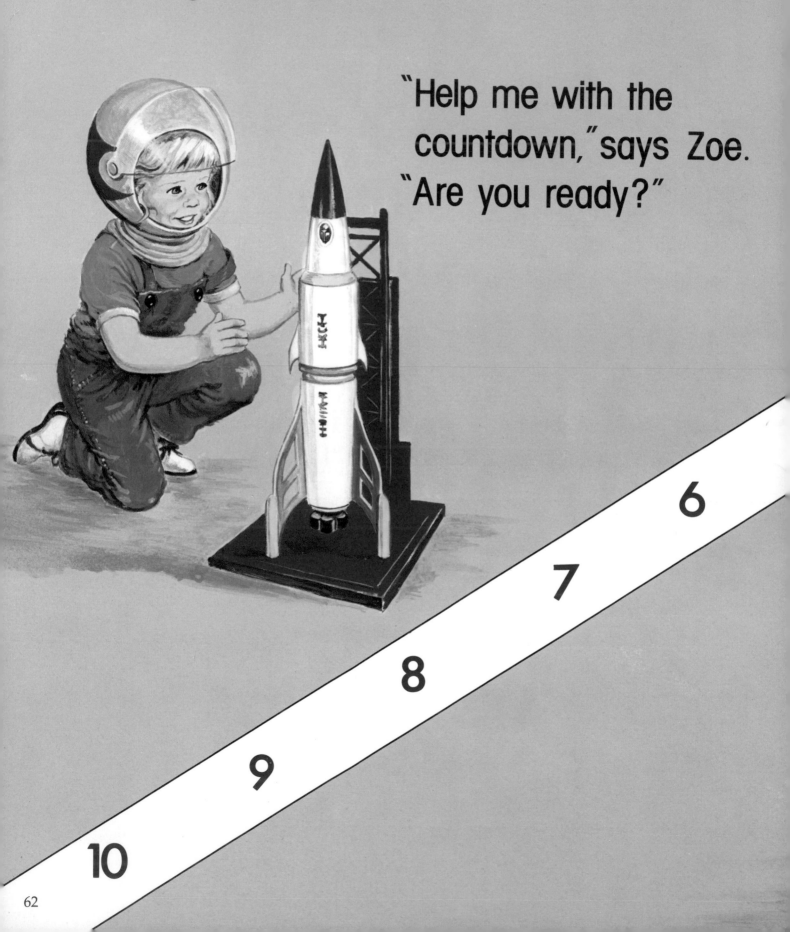

6

7

8

9

10

"We have lift off!"
says Alex."We are
off to the moon."

Let's make a long train.

1st   2nd   3rd   4th

"I am first, I am the driver," says Zoe.

5th 6th 7th 8th 9th 10th

"I am last, I am the guard," says Alex.

Say this counting rhyme with us

One red engine puffing down the track
One red engine puffing puffing back

Two blue engines puffing down the track
Two blue engines puffing puffing back

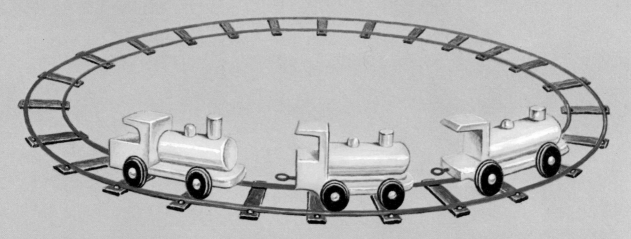

Three yellow engines puffing down the track
Three yellow engines puffing puffing back

Four green engines puffing down the track
Four green engines puffing puffing back

Five orange engines puffing down the track
Five orange engines puffing puffing back

We are sorting our toys

Zoe has put together...

3				cars
2				planes
4				boats
3				balls

68

Alex has sorted the toys into...

4	**blue**	✈	🪁	🚐	🚗	
3	**green**	⚫	⬛	🚗		
4	**yellow**	🦆	🛒	📘	🚚	
5	**red**	☕	🪣	⚫	yo-yo	shovel

More sorting

We can put our bricks

In 2's

In 3's

In 4's

In 5's

Join in our counting rhyme

There were 10 in the bed...

There were 9 in the bed...

And the little one said,
"Roll over, roll over!"
So they all rolled over
And one fell out.

There were 8 in the bed...

There were 7 in the bed...

There were **6** in the bed...

There were **5** in the bed...

And the little one said,
"Roll over, roll over!"
So they all rolled over
And one fell out.

There were **4** in the bed...

There were **3** in the bed

There were **2** in the bed...
And the little one said,
"Roll over, roll over!"
So they rolled over
And one fell out.

There was **1** in the bed
And the little one said,
"Roll over, roll over!"
So she rolled over
And she fell out.

There were none in the bed
And no one said,
"Roll over, roll over!"

"We are all down here!"
How many on the floor?

Find out with us !
WORDS

A Guide to **WORDS**

WORDS provides a valuable aid which enables children to describe their own experiences and the world around them by the use of words and pictures. The picture clues help children to use words, even if at first, they cannot read them.

The first section is alphabetically presented for easy word location and to emphasize the sounds of letters. It also contains subjects that a child might see, draw and subsequently want to write about. The sections which follow show the child in progressive steps how to begin to write, simple linking and descriptive words; characters in stories; actions; plurals; numbers etc.

WORDS will help to extend vocabulary, develop writing skill and open up the exciting world of written language at any stage of early learning. Shown how to use the examples given, children will return to these pages again to discover new words and the fun of creative writing by themselves.

Looking for words

"How can I write 'house'?"
says Zoe.
"I will turn the pages and look
for 'h'," says Alex.

Aa

Bb

alligator	ant	ambulance
apple	astronaut	airport
ball	boat	bicycle
bus	bed	bird

Cc   Dd

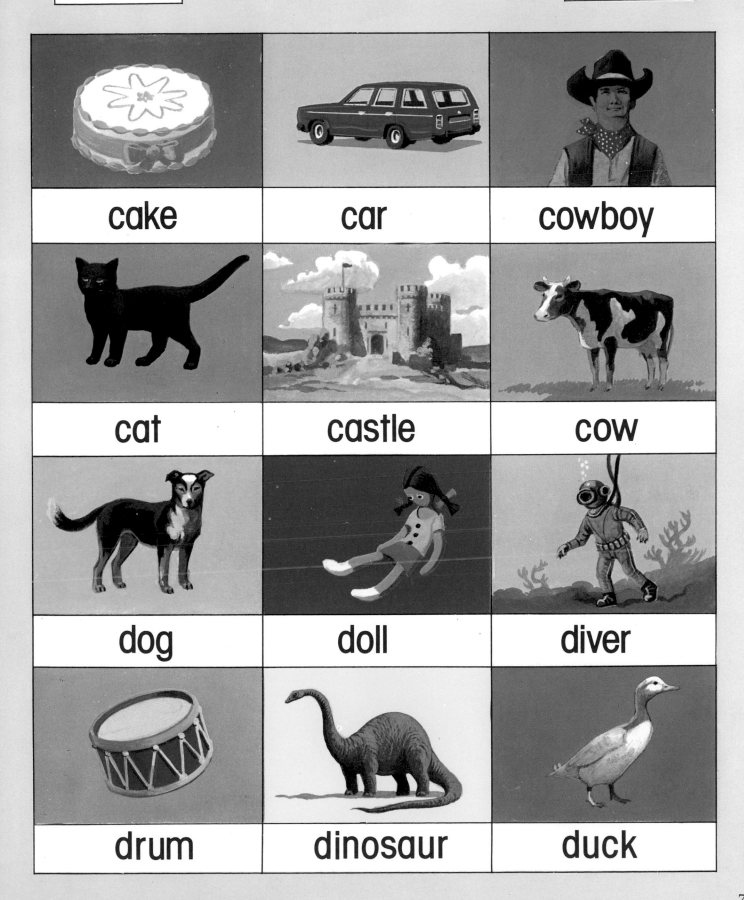

cake	car	cowboy
cat	castle	cow
dog	doll	diver
drum	dinosaur	duck

crocodile	crown	clown
crane	crab	clock
donkey	door	dress
dolphin	driver	desk

Ee		**Ff**
egg	elephant	eskimo
envelope	eagle	emu
fire-engine	fish	flag
flowers	fruit	frog

garage	garden	gloves
grapes	giraffe	gorilla
helicopter	house	hospital
hammer	horse	hamster

Indian	igloo	ice cream
island	insect	iron
jigsaw	jellyfish	jeans
jet plane	jaguar	jug

kangaroo	kite	key
kettle	kitten	kitchen
lion	leaves	lollipop
ladybird	lighthouse	lemon

moon	monkey	motorcycle
mouse	mask	milk
nest	night	nuts
newspaper	necklace	net

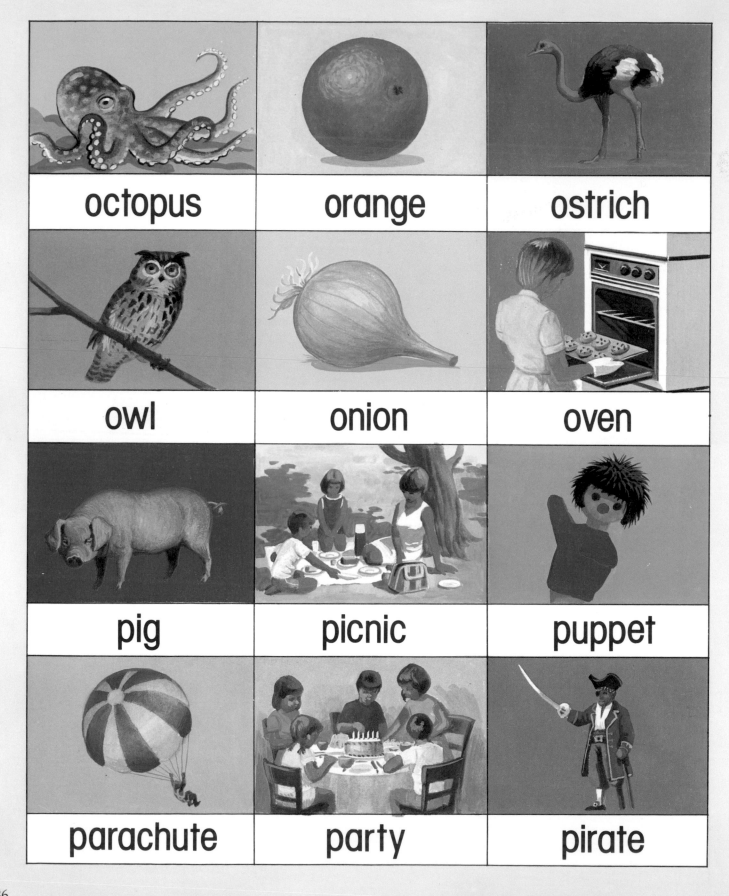

octopus	orange	ostrich
owl	onion	oven
pig	picnic	puppet
parachute	party	pirate

Qq

Rr

quarter	quilt	quads
quail	quarrel	quiet
rabbit	rocket	rose
radio	robin	racing car

87

Ss		**Tt**

snake	spaceship	sun
submarine	school	shark
telephone	tree	train
television	tortoise	tiger

Uu   Vv

umbrella	unicorn	under
upside down	upstairs	umpire
visit	vegetables	volcano
violin	vulture	valentine

water	woods	whale
wedding	watch	wasp
x-ray	xylophone	boxer
fox	box	ox

Not many words begin with X – Here are some words with X
in the middle or at the end.

yacht	yolk	yo-yo
yawn	yak	yard
zebra	zip	zig-zag

zoo

Ways to begin to write

Here is a _ _ _ _ _

This is my _ _ _ _ _

I can see _ _ _ _ _

I went to _ _ _ _ _

First draw a picture. Choose one line on this page to begin writing.
Look for other words you need in the pages of this book.

Little words we can use

it	me	at	up
is	my	an	he
on	we	am	do
to	us	go	if

and	had	she	out
the	saw	you	new
are	his	get	fun
has	her	for	our

they	like	into	look
make	made	with	help
went	dear	love	from
some	down	said	none

Ways to start a story

Once upon a time there was _ _ _ _ _

Long long ago there lived _ _ _ _ _

One day _ _ _ _ _

In the land of _ _ _ _ _

First draw a picture. Choose one line on this page to begin your story. Look for other words you need in the pages of this book.

king | queen | prince | princess

witch | wizard | ghost | giant

dragon | fairy | mermaid | elf

More than one....

one house

two houses

girls

boys

toys

What they are like

big	little	fat	thin
old	new	hot	cold
good	wicked	happy	sad

in	out	fast	slow
thick	thin	empty	full
light	heavy	tall	short

old	young	straight	crooked
ugly	pretty	more	less
wet	dry	up	down

Making a rainbow

red	blue	yellow	green	orange
purple	brown	pink	black	white

Numbers

one 1	two 2	three 3	four 4
five 5	six 6	seven 7	
eight 8	nine 9	ten 10	

Our family

Zoe is my sister	Alex is my brother
Alex	Zoe

Mother	Father
Grandmother	Grandfather
Aunt	Uncle
cousins	baby

Things we can do...

We like this game.

It is fun.

We take turns to throw

the hoops at the target.

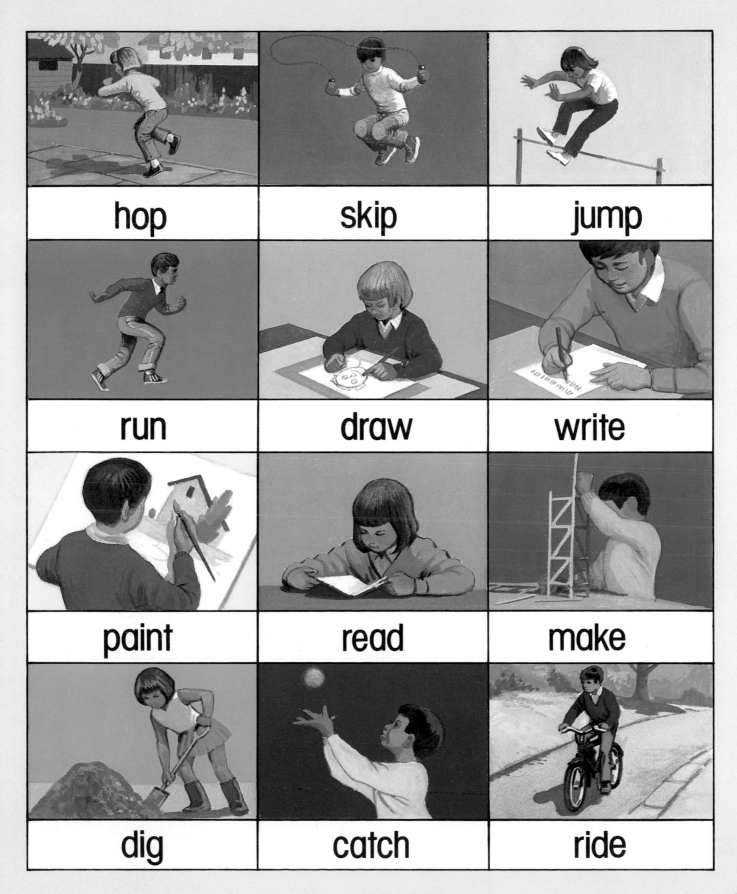

hop	skip	jump
run	draw	write
paint	read	make
dig	catch	ride

Places to go...

We like to go to the beach.

We can play on the beach

with our friends.

We can make sand castles.

zoo

park

playground

farm

library

fair

The weather

Looking out of the window.

We can see it is raining.

The water drips and splashes.

It makes puddles.

snowing

foggy

sunny

windy

frosty

stormy

109

People we know

We can play a game.

Alex is the doctor.

Zoe is the nurse.

Teddy is ill. We can make him better.

fireman

teacher

painter

farmer

dentist

builder

Which day is it?

Yesterday was Sunday

Today is Monday

Tomorrow will be Tuesday

Wednesday

Thursday

Friday

Saturday

morning **afternoon** **evening**

In one day we....

get up	wash	dress
eat	work	play
watch	undress	bath
listen	go to bed	sleep

This is my ball

The dog is running

114

Here is a fish

Our cat is black

My blue car

115

Look with us at
ANIMALS

A Guide to **ANIMALS**

Animals are a fascinating part of our world. In these pages, children can discover and learn about domestic, wild, rare and exotic species depicted in their natural surroundings.

In the first section are shown familiar pets, followed by animals found in the garden, on the seashore and on the farm. These are places known to many children where they are able to come into close contact with animals. They can touch, watch and form relationships with them.

Wild animals are less accessible. A large section introduces them grouped according to their own environment—hot lands, jungles, deserts, cold lands, woodlands, forests, mountains and seas.

The illustrations provide a realistic view of more than a hundred living creatures, what they look like; where and how they live.

The simply worded text conveys a wealth of interesting facts about animals at an easy reading level.

Buying a pet.

Our puppy needs...

food and water

baths and brushing

walks and play

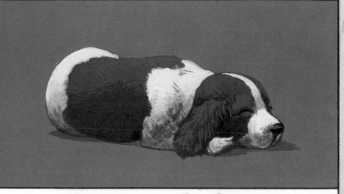

plenty of sleep

and lots of love.

cat

rabbit

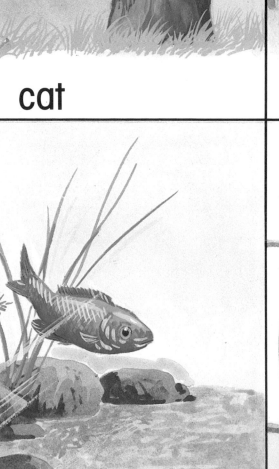

goldfish

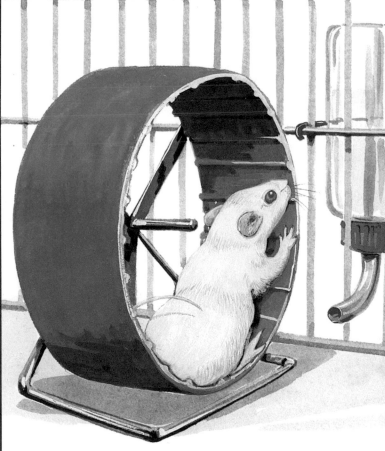

mouse

guinea pig

tortoise

budgerigar

hamster

In the garden.

spider and web

earwigs

snails

ladybirds

woodlice

worms

butterfly

sparrow

ants

caterpillars

On the seashore.

seagulls

limpets

hermit crabs

crabs

periwinkles

sea urchins

anemones

whelks

starfish

mussels

124

On the farm.

cow

donkey

horse

dog

sheep

chickens

Families and babies.

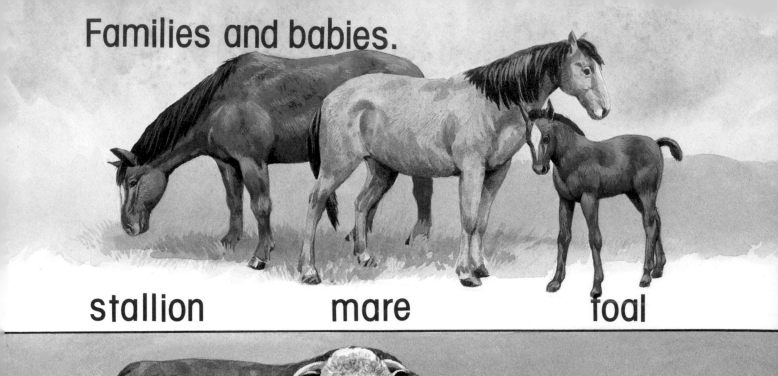

stallion   mare   foal

bull   cow   calf

billy-goat   nanny-goat   kid

cockerel   hen   chick

boar   sow   piglet

ram   ewe   lamb

drake   **duck**   **duckling**

buck   **doe**   **fawn**

lion   **lioness**   **cub**

Some animals with pouches

sugar glider

opossum

kangaroo

koala

wombat

Tasmanian devil

hen

cat

horse

donkey

sheep

cow

pig goat duck

"My animals live with people.
They are tame."

elephant

zebra

tiger

lion

buffalo

polar bear

fox

kangaroo

stoat

"My animals live free all over the world. They are wild."

puma — mountain lion
—cougar

lynx

jaguar

leopard

lion

132

The tiger's stripes hide him in the long grass.
He likes to swim but never climbs trees.

The cheetah has long legs. He can run faster
than any other animal.

In the hot grassland.

buffalo

zebra

stork

Grant's gazelle

giraffe

ostrich

rhinoceros

warthog

hyena

The <u>elephants</u> are cool in the water. They squirt water with their trunks.

The <u>giraffe</u> curls its long tongue round the leaves at the top of the tree.

Mother <u>crocodile</u> is gentle as she takes her babies into the water.

The baby <u>hippopotamus</u> is born under the water. He loves to be wet and muddy.

The <u>anteater</u> licks up the ants. He cannot open his mouth and he has no teeth.

The <u>flamingoes</u> feed with their heads upsidedown and their bills in the water.

These <u>camels</u> have two humps and long shaggy hair.
They live in the **desert**.

The <u>Gila-monster</u> is a poisonous lizard. He moves
slowly in the hot sun.

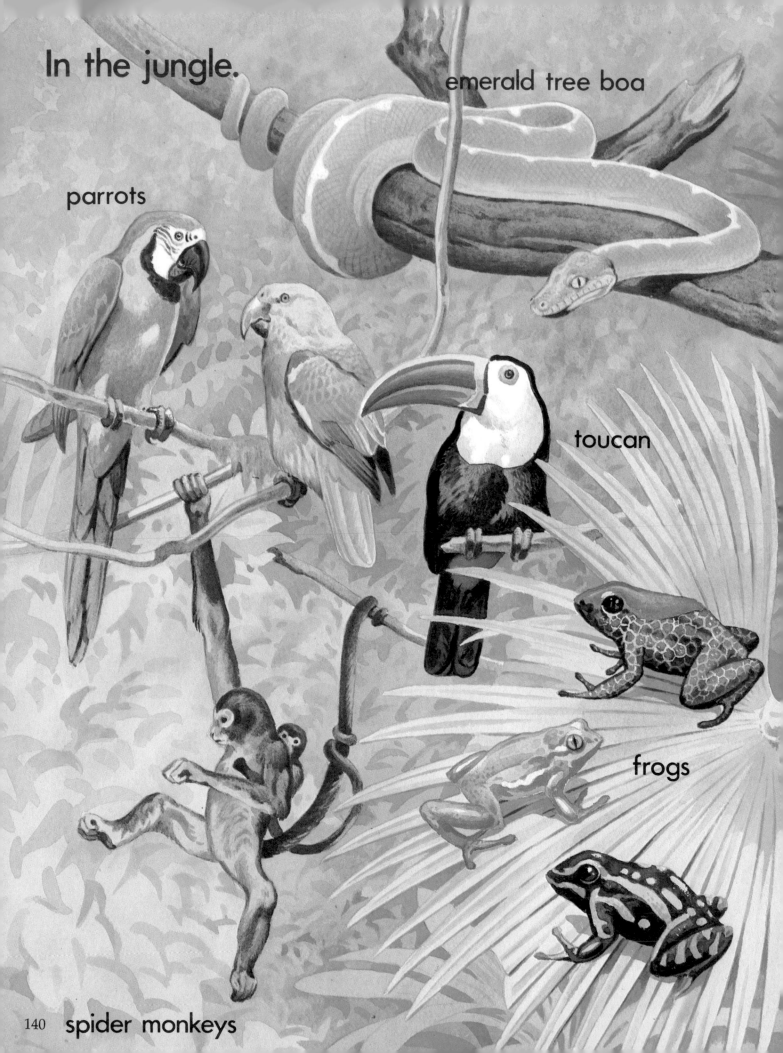

In the jungle.

emerald tree boa

parrots

toucan

frogs

spider monkeys

The orang-utan walks slowly along the branches. He does not swing or jump.

The gorillas are big and strong. They are also quiet and gentle.

The <u>chimpanzee</u> has a drink. He does not play in the water and cannot swim.

The <u>chameleon</u> lives in trees. He uses his long sticky tongue to catch food.

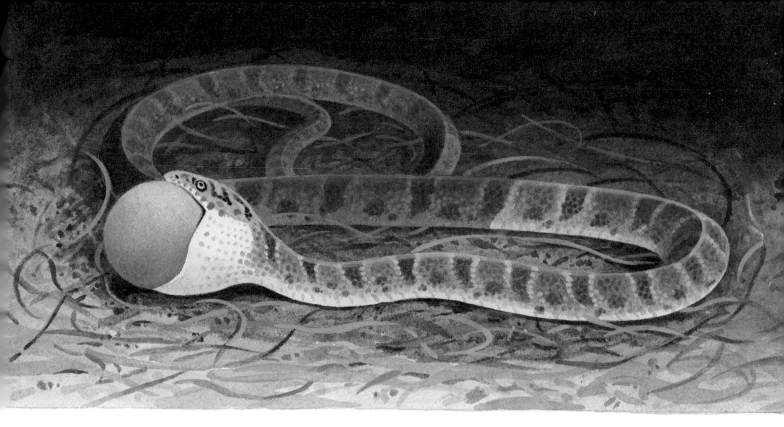

This egg-eating <u>snake</u> has no teeth. He swallows the egg and spits out the shell.

The giant <u>panda</u> eats bamboo. He lives in the forest high in the mountains.

In the cold lands.

musk oxen

grey wolves

arctic fox

arctic hare

reindeer

seals

145

Mother <u>polar bear</u> keeps her cubs warm in their den under the snow.

The <u>walrus</u> uses its tusks to climb out of the water and up the ice.

The <u>sea-lions</u> use their flippers to swim
and to move on the ice.

Father <u>penguin</u> keeps the baby chick warm.
Mother hunts in the water for food.

In a storm the mother <u>yaks</u> will make a circle round their babies to keep them warm.

In the winter the <u>moose</u> digs away the snow with his hooves to find food.

The big-horn sheep have thick woolly coats
to keep them warm in the winter.

The golden eagle carries sticks back to its
nest high in the mountains.

In the woods.

red squirrel

grey squirrel

owl

fox

weasel

stoat

hedgehog

The <u>badgers</u> live under the ground. At night they come out
to look for food.

The <u>moles</u> dig tunnels with their front paws. They are
looking for worms.

In the forest.

brown bear

porcupine

racoon

rattlesnake

skunk

chipmunk

The <u>otter's</u> long whiskers help him to feel his way through the muddy water.

The <u>beaver</u> uses his strong teeth to chop down the trees to make his home.

The <u>prairie dog</u> is on guard. He will warn the
others if there is danger.

The <u>black bear</u> cubs stay up in the tree when
mother bear goes hunting.

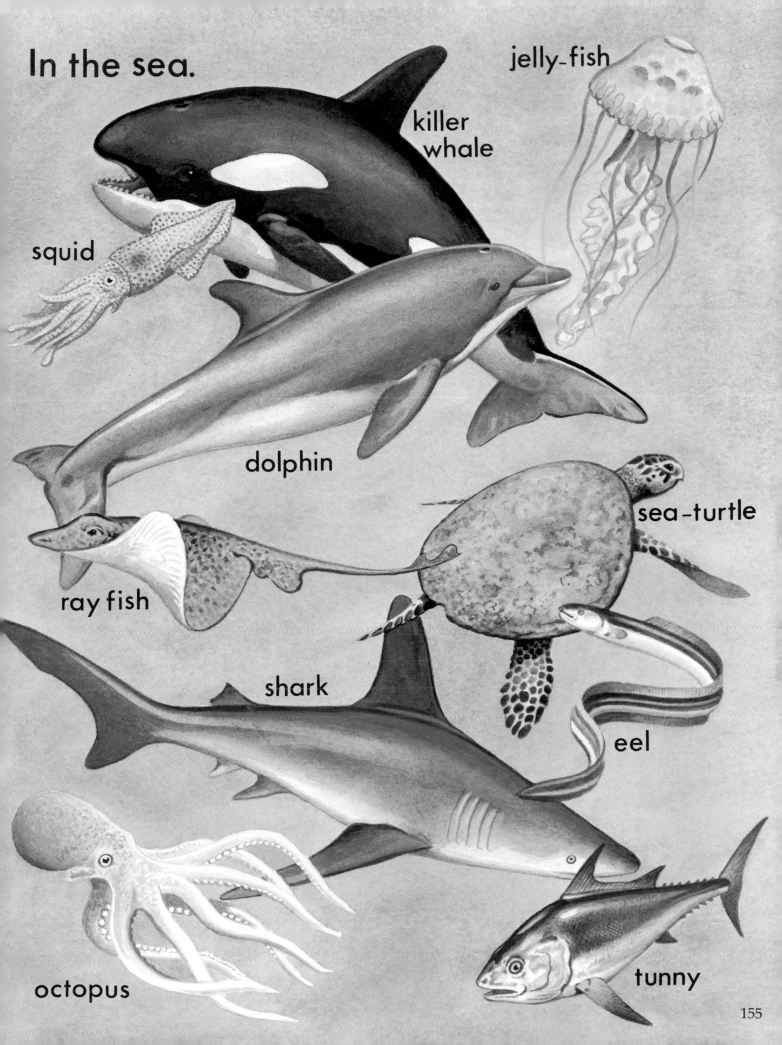

In the sea.

killer whale

jelly-fish

squid

dolphin

sea-turtle

ray fish

shark

eel

octopus

tunny

155

Do you know?

The blue whale is the biggest of all the animals.

The ostrich is the biggest bird — but it cannot fly.

The biggest
animal on land
is the elephant.

A giraffe
sleeps standing up.